WHAT'S happening TO ME?

Micaela Tapsell
Illustrated by Camille Ferrari

Designed by: Neil Francis

WITH EXPERT ADVICE FROM:
Laura Clarke, sex educator
Dr Anna Forringer-Beal, gender studies researcher
Dr Caitríona Cox, medical doctor

CONTENTS

GROWING UP	3
WHEN WILL PUBERTY BEGIN?	4
TALLER AND WIDER	6
GETTING HAIRY	8
GETTING BREASTS	10
DOWN THERE	14
CHANGES ON THE INSIDE	16
WHAT IS A PERIOD?	18
FEELING HORMONAL	28
YOU AND YOUR GENDER	30
WHAT ABOUT BOYS?	34
EXPLORING YOUR BODY	37
HAVING CRUSHES	38
YOUR BODY, YOUR RULES	40
WHAT ACTUALLY IS SEX?	42
SAFE SEX	44
BEING ONLINE	46
FUELLING YOUR BODY	50
KEEP CLEAN	52
OLDER AND WISER	54
YOUR SUPPORT CREW	56
BECOMING YOU	58
GLOSSARY	60
INDEX	62

GROWING UP

You've been growing up little by little ever since you were born, but there's a time when you'll start to change a lot. That's when you begin to grow from a child into an adult, and it's what this book is all about.

You might have noticed some changes happening to you already, or maybe there haven't been any yet. They don't happen to everyone at the same age, or in the same way, and you can't tell in advance when they'll happen to you. But this book will give you a good idea of what to expect.

This new phase in your life is called puberty. It's all to do with growing up and preparing your body for adulthood. Perhaps you're looking forward to growing up, or maybe you have doubts. Don't worry – the changes take place gradually, so you'll have plenty of time to get used to them.

WHEN WILL PUBERTY BEGIN?

People usually say you start changing when you're about 10, but it happens to some people earlier than this and to others quite a bit later. The fact is, when your body is ready, you'll start growing up.

GEARING UP

First of all, you have to build up some fat. This is a healthy way for your body to store the energy it needs for the changes ahead.

Everyone grows up at their own pace. You might be the same age as your friends, but you could finish developing before they start, or the other way around.

You can't make yourself grow up faster, or more slowly. But one thing's for sure – everyone gets to the same stage in the end. No matter how old you are when you start puberty, you'll go on changing until you're fully grown up.

WHAT NEXT?

Just so you know what to expect, here are some changes you're likely to experience. Don't worry if you don't recognize some of these words – they'll all be explained later in the book.

- Your pubic hair starts to grow.
- Hair grows under your arms.
- You start to sweat more.
- Your face gets longer.
- You get taller, broader and heavier.
- Your skin and hair may get greasier.
- Your sex organs develop.
- Your breasts start to develop.
- Your periods start.

It can take up to 3½ years from the very first changes of puberty to starting your periods. And it will be several more years after that before you finish growing up. All along, you'll start to feel a bit different in yourself. Don't worry though; you'll still be you at the end of it all – just a more grown-up version of yourself.

Me, age 5

TALLER AND WIDER

When everyone starts telling you how much you've grown, the chances are that other changes are on the way too. Once you're a little taller, you'll probably start broadening out as well. Not everyone has a really obvious growth spurt. Some seem to grow more gradually over several years.

Hey! Standing on tiptoes is cheating.

A GROWTH SPURT

You usually grow fastest around the time you're 11½, but you may grow tall when you're quite a bit younger or older than this. You might be nearly finished growing by the time you're 15.

If you go through a growth spurt early, it's likely that you'll stop growing early too. And if you start your growth spurt later, you may well catch up with the early growers and even overtake them.

THE BROAD BITS

The bones of your pelvis widen during puberty which causes your hips to broaden out. Some people notice their shoulders becoming wider too.

MUSCLE POWER

All your muscles get bigger during puberty, including the ones you can't see – such as your heart and lungs. Your voice box, which sits in your neck, also grows bigger and thicker. This will make your voice slightly deeper over time.

GETTING BIGGER

You'll probably double in weight between the ages of 9 and 18. Part of that is growing taller: your bones get bigger, you get more fat and muscle, and your organs – such as your stomach and liver – get bigger too. Female bodies tend to put on more fat than male bodies, but it's normal for everyone to gain weight during puberty.

GETTING HAIRY

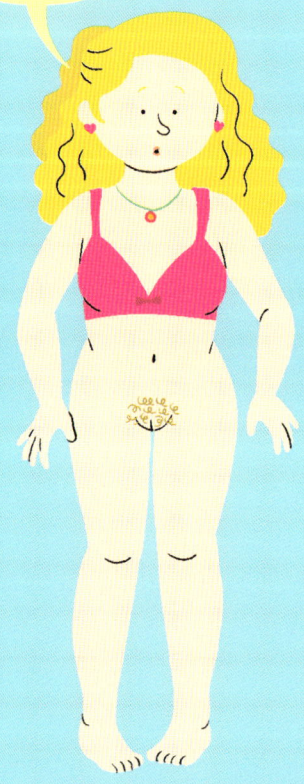

Well this is new.

During puberty, you'll start getting hair in places you didn't have it before. The hair is natural and everybody gets it.

PUBIC HAIR

Pubic hair can grow around your genitals, on your lower stomach, inner thighs and between your bum cheeks. It gets more curly as it grows, and might be a different colour to the hair on your head. Some people choose to trim it or shave it, while others don't.

UNDER YOUR ARMS

About a year after you get pubic hair, you'll notice hair starts growing in your armpits too. It's up to you what to do with it. Some people keep it while others choose to remove it, either by shaving or waxing. If you decide to shave and notice that your armpits feel a bit sore, it may be that your blade is blunt or that you're sensitive to the foam you're using.

ON YOUR LEGS

It's normal to get more hair on your legs too. Humans are related to apes so it's no wonder we're hairy. Body hair is natural and clean, so it's up to you whether you want to keep it or not. If you choose to shave your legs, go slowly in an upwards direction towards your body. Only shave your legs if you want to – you don't have to do it, and lots of people choose not to.

Shaving your legs is SO last season.

DEODORANTS

Many people put deodorant on their armpits at the start of each day, to stop smells developing when they sweat. Some deodorants, called anti-perspirants, also cut down on *how much* you sweat. Using deodorant on your armpits is a good idea, especially when you're exercising, but you don't have to use one. Just remember that they aren't a substitute for washing!

Meow!

GETTING BREASTS

During puberty, your breasts will start to grow. When this happens, you might notice a small bump behind your nipple, about the size of a blueberry. This is called a breast bud, and it's a sign that your boobs are on their way! Everyone develops at different rates, and your breasts can carry on growing until you're about 17.

GROWING PAINS

As your breasts start to grow, they might feel a bit sore, tingly or itchy, but this will wear off. One breast may grow faster than the other, but they'll even out eventually – although no one has exactly symmetrical breasts. Your breasts will continue to change during adulthood too. Changes in your weight can make your breasts bigger or smaller, and they may also feel different or more sensitive from day to day.

BREASTS AND MILK

Breasts are able to produce milk – but only after a baby is born. It comes out of the nipples through tiny holes that are too small to see.

To cushion and protect the milk-making areas, breasts are mostly made of fat.

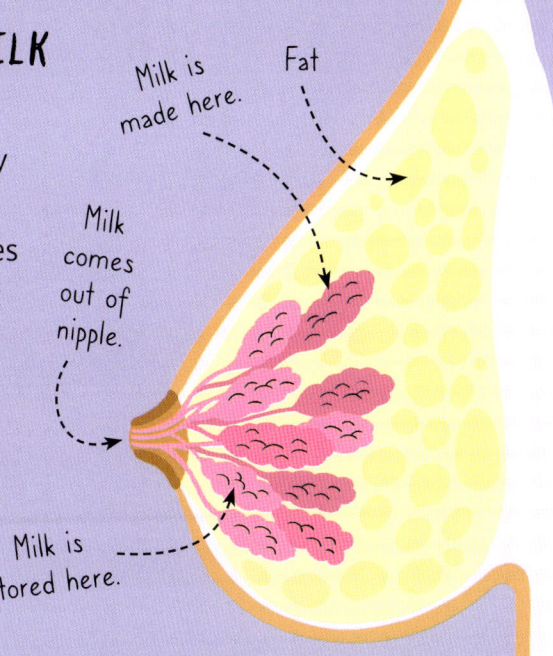

Milk is made here.

Fat

Milk comes out of nipple.

Milk is stored here.

The shape and size of breasts and nipples differ from person to person – ALL of them are normal.

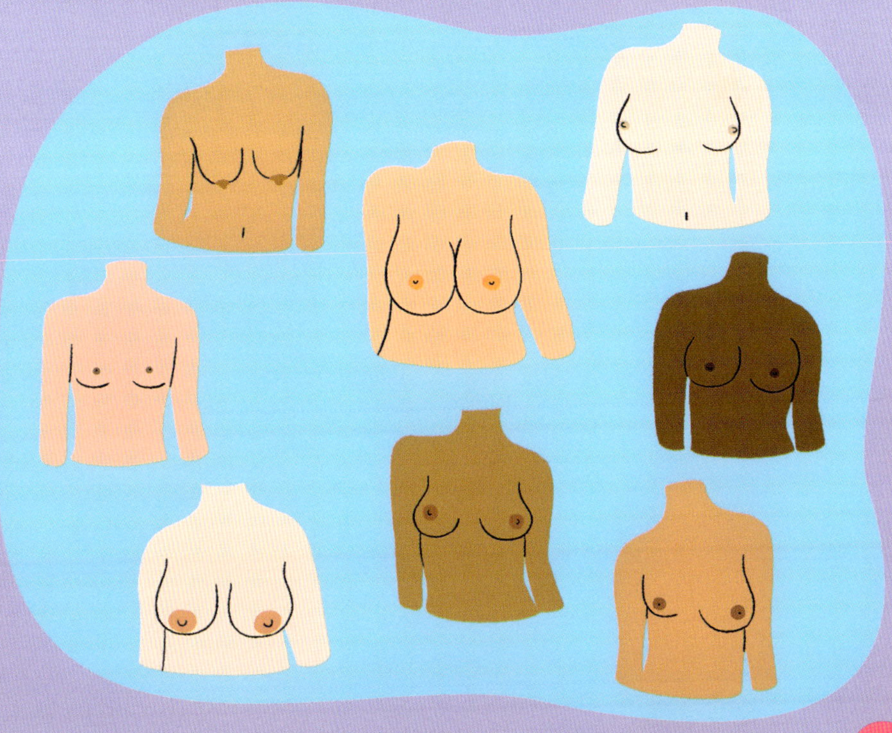

BRA BUSINESS

Some people wear a bra to support their breasts, but it's up to you if you want to wear one or not. There are bras for all different sizes, big and small.

THE RIGHT FIT

The only way to find a bra that really fits is to try on different sizes – it's a bit of trial and error. The correct bra should fit tightly around your ribs so that it can't ride up, and should support your breasts without squashing them against your chest. You may need to adjust the straps to feel more comfortable.

THE WRONG FIT

There are a few ways to know if your bra isn't the right fit for your breasts. If your bra slips down, looks wrinkly around the front or unhooks on its own at the back, then it's probably too big. If your bra digs in at the front, rides up at the back or causes your breasts to spill out the side by your armpit, then it's probably too small. Some stores offer a breast measuring service to help you figure out your bra size.

...or should I wear this one instead?

TYPES OF BRA

'First' or 'teen' bras are made to be soft and comfortable. They usually cover your breasts completely.

SPORTS BRA

Supports your breasts and keeps you cool while you exercise.

T-SHIRT BRA

Sits comfortably under a top, without lots of seams or decoration.

FRONT CLASP BRA

Hooks at the front, between the breasts, so it's easy to put on.

MULTIWAY BRA

Adjustable straps that can be hidden when you wear halterneck or other style tops.

UNDERWIRED BRA

Gives extra support for larger breasts.

My first bra!

DOWN THERE

A big part of puberty is the changes that happen to your sex organs, including your private parts. People often avoid talking about them, or use funny words to describe them. Here are the proper names for them:

YOUR VULVA

The vulva is the name for your bits *down there*. It's made up of different parts, including two thick folds of skin called the outer labia (lips). Inside the outer labia you have two smaller lips called the inner labia. These are sensitive to touch.

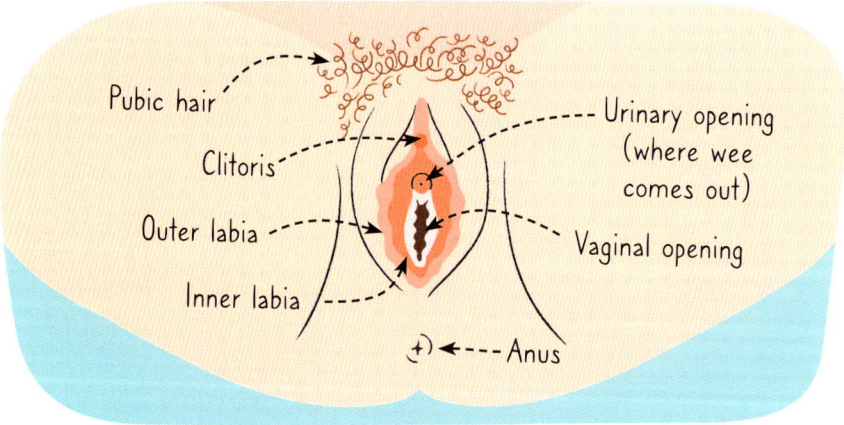

At the front, where your inner labia meet, is a pea-shaped bump called the clitoris. This is very sensitive to touch.

Your vagina is a tube that goes a few inches inside your body. It has an opening that can stretch, and it may be surrounded by a thin layer of skin called the hymen. This usually wears away over time as you grow.

NEARBY PARTS

The tiny hole where your urine comes out, called the urinary opening, is a bit further back than your clitoris. Your anus (where poo comes out) isn't part of your vulva either, but it's very close to it.

THE SAME, BUT DIFFERENT

Pubic hair and genitals look different from person to person – they can be all sorts of shapes and sizes. You can use a mirror to see what your genitals look like if you want to.

CHANGES ON THE INSIDE

There are sex organs inside your body, too. As you grow, these also change – though you won't notice straight away.

WHERE EVERYTHING IS

Your sex organs (shown below in red) are low down below your tummy, behind and just above your bladder, where urine (wee) is stored. They are protected by the bones of your pelvis.

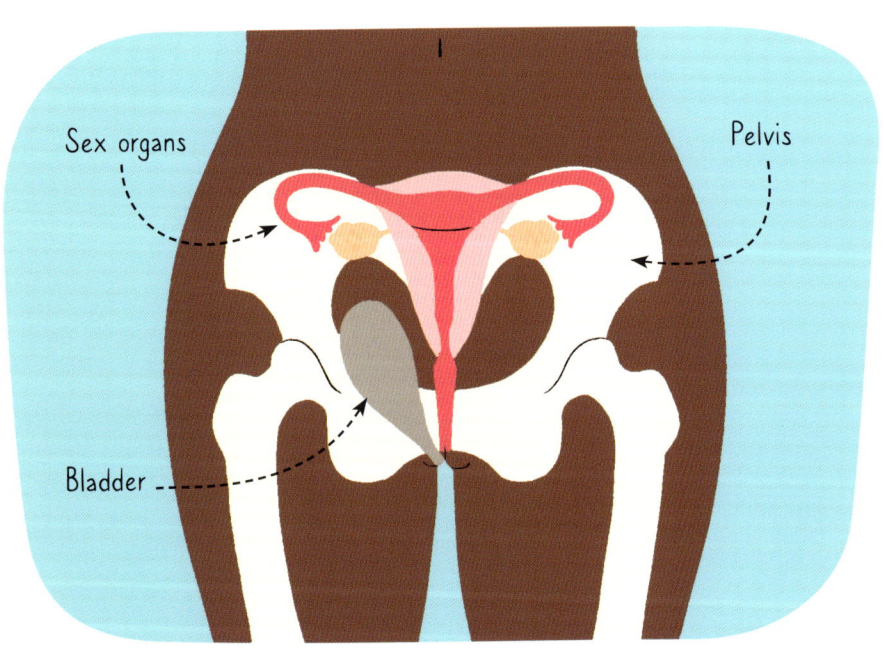

WHAT'S ON THE INSIDE

You have two ovaries, two fallopian tubes, a uterus (also called a womb), a cervix and a vagina. These will all get bigger, just like the rest of you.

The hollow part of your fallopian tubes is only about as wide as the lead in a pencil.

Your ovaries are where things called eggs are stored. When your ovaries are fully grown, they are about the size and shape of walnuts.

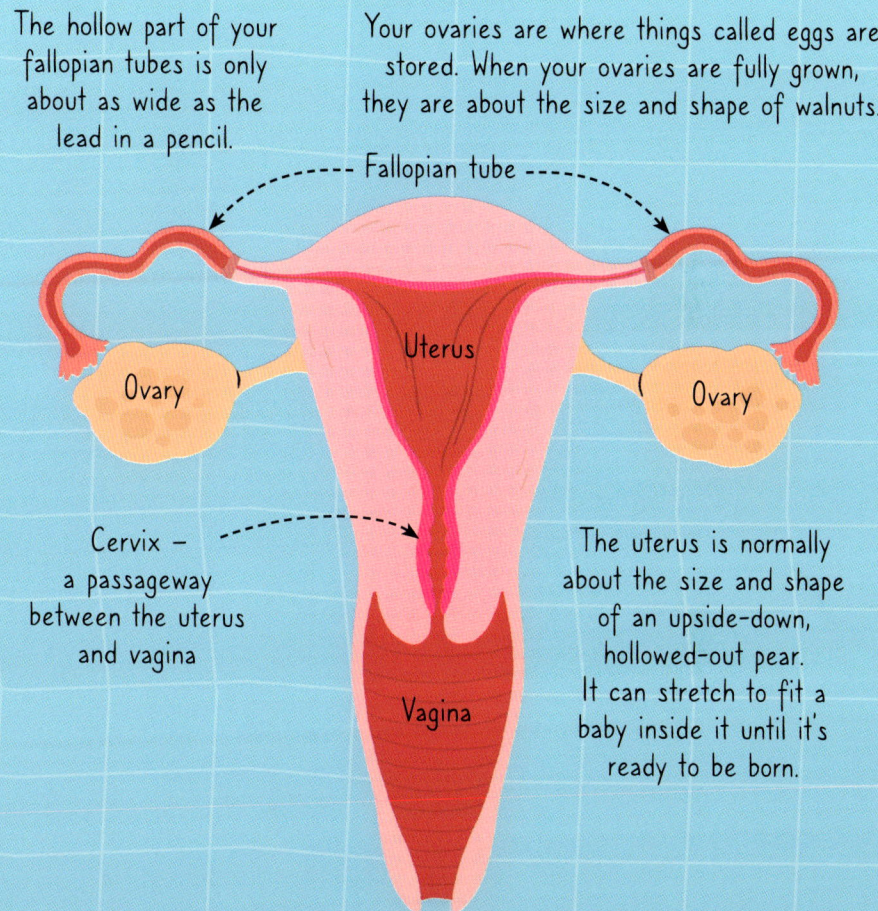

Cervix – a passageway between the uterus and vagina

The uterus is normally about the size and shape of an upside-down, hollowed-out pear. It can stretch to fit a baby inside it until it's ready to be born.

Your vagina is a tube which leads to the outside of your body. It is about 10cm (4in) long and its walls are very stretchy. Each day, a small amount of whitish fluid will come out of your vagina. This is called discharge, and it keeps your vagina clean. About once a month, blood will come out of your vagina, for something called a period. This is what the next few pages are all about.

WHAT IS A PERIOD?

The biggest growing-up change of all is when your period starts. A period is when blood comes out of your vagina for a few days each month.

PERIODS AND BABIES

Every month, the womb builds up a thick, soft lining of blood vessels. This is so that, one day, a baby *could* nestle there and grow. Unless a person becomes pregnant, the womb lining breaks down and comes out of their vagina as a period.

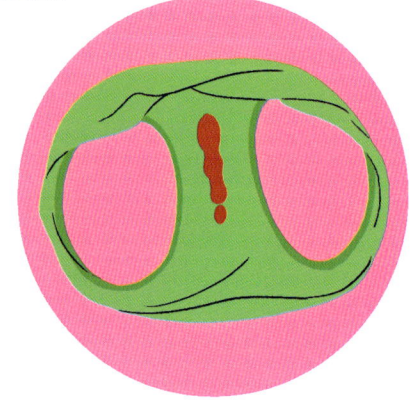

People usually notice a period has started when they go to the toilet.

WHEN PERIODS START

There are a couple of clues that tell you when your periods might be about to start. It will probably be about 2½ years after your breasts begin to grow. For a few months before your first period, you might get more fluid than usual coming out of your vagina. Periods usually start sometime between the ages of 10 and 15 – but some start younger.

When will I get my period?

Mine started when I was 12.

HEAVY OR LIGHT?

Roughly six tablespoons of blood comes out of the vagina during an average period. But everyone is different. You might have a light period, which means you don't bleed much, or a heavy one, which means you bleed quite a lot. Both cases are normal.

You will also find that your period is generally heavier in the first few days and lighter at the end. Period blood can be lots of different shades, from bright red at the start to dark brown at the end. Over time, you'll get to know your body better and learn what to expect.

A WAITING GAME

A period often comes at around the same time each month. This is known as a regular period, because it sticks to a regular schedule. A period can also be irregular, meaning it comes slightly earlier or later than you're expecting.

Sometimes, you might notice a little bit of blood in between your periods, either in your knickers or when you go to the toilet. This is called spotting, and it's normal too.

It's a good idea to carry period products with you in case you need them when you're not expecting it. You can read about these in the next few pages.

USING PERIOD PADS

Many people choose to use pads when they first start their period. Period pads fit in your knickers and soak up the blood as it leaves your body. You can buy pads from any supermarket, but most schools will have some that they can give you for free if you need them.

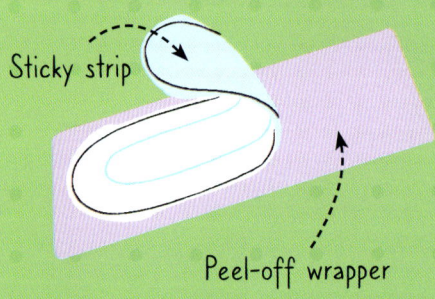

Sticky strip

Peel-off wrapper

TYPES OF PADS

Pads have a sticky strip on the back so that they stay in place once you press them into your knickers. Some have side flaps too, known as wings. These fold over and stick to the underneath of your knickers, to make them extra secure.

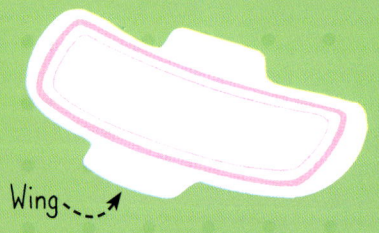

Wing

SIZE AND THICKNESS

Pads come in different sizes and thicknesses. You might need a thicker pad at the start of your period and at bedtime, when you won't be changing it until the morning.

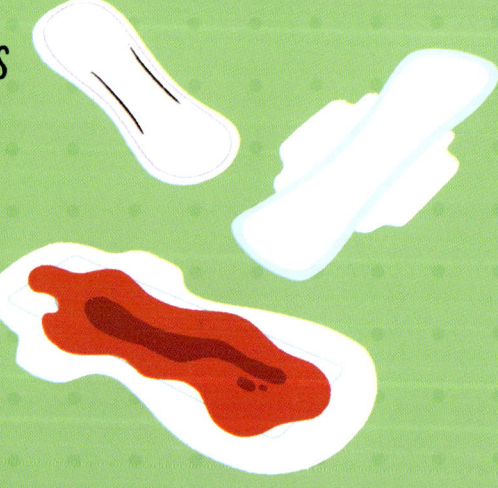

CHANGING PADS

You'll soon learn how to tell when your pad needs changing. In the day, you should change pads every few hours – not just in case they leak, but also to stop bacteria building up. Period blood is completely clean, but when it's outside your body for a long time, it meets bacteria in the air and might cause a smell.

GETTING RID OF PADS

You can't flush pads down the toilet. Instead, you need to wrap them up and put them in a bin. If your pads are individually wrapped, you can put them back in their wrapper to throw away; or you can buy sanitary disposal bags. It's a good idea to take a bag with you when you go out, although special bins are often provided in public toilets.

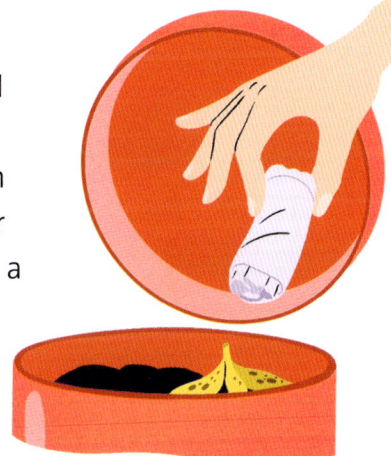

QUICKLINKS

You might find it helpful to watch some videos online that show you how to use period products. Turn to page 63 for some suggestions.

USING TAMPONS

Tampons are soft plugs of fabric that can be put up into the vagina to soak up period blood. You shouldn't feel a tampon once it's in place. If you *can* feel it, then you probably need to push it up a little bit further until you find a comfortable spot.

TYPES OF TAMPONS

Some tampons come with an applicator designed to help you insert the tampon.

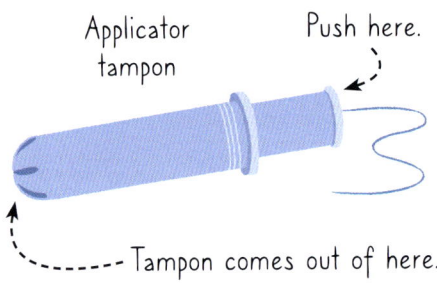

Applicator tampon

Push here.

Tampon comes out of here.

There are also non-applicator types of tampons, which you just push in with your finger.

Non-applicator tampon

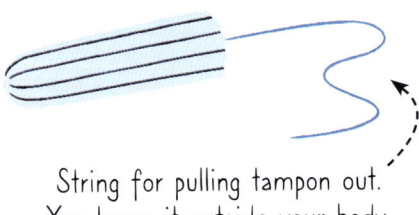

String for pulling tampon out. You leave it outside your body.

Tampons come in different sizes. The size you use depends on how heavy your period is, not on the size of your body. Some packs have a few tampons of different sizes in them, for different days of your period.

Mini size for when a period is light.

Regular size for in-between days.

Super size for when a period is heavy.

PUTTING A TAMPON IN

It's best to try a tampon for the first time when your period is heavy, as it will go in more easily. Use a small size, and follow the instructions. You might find it helpful to squat, or to put one leg up on the toilet, as you put the tampon in. It does take a bit of practice. It's okay if you can't get it in after a few tries. Leave it and try again another time.

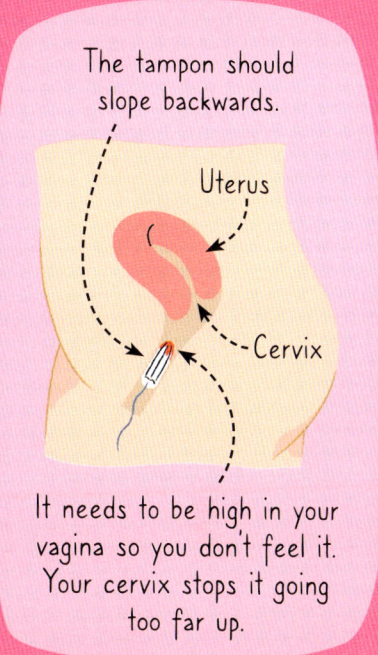

The tampon should slope backwards.

Uterus

Cervix

It needs to be high in your vagina so you don't feel it. Your cervix stops it going too far up.

CHANGING TAMPONS

Changing your tampon every four hours or sooner will keep you healthy and feeling comfortable. Leaving a tampon in for much longer than this can cause an infection called toxic shock syndrome. It's very rare, but you should still get into the good habit of changing your tampons regularly. You could use a period pad at night, so that you don't leave a tampon in for too long while you sleep. Tampons should be thrown away in a bin, not in a toilet.

PERIOD PANTS

Period pants look like regular underwear, except they have a special absorbent layer that stops your menstrual blood from leaking through to your clothing. You can wear and wash them again and again. But you'd probably need to own a few different pairs to get you through your whole period.

Look, I'm not going to do your laundry for you forever you know.

Inner lining

They come with different levels of absorbencies, depending on how heavy your period is. If your periods are particularly heavy, you might feel comfortable using them alongside other period products too. You should change your period pants every four to six hours or so.

MENSTRUAL CUPS

A menstrual cup is soft and bendy, so that you can fold and insert it into your vagina, where it sits and collects your blood. You can keep a menstrual cup inside your vagina for up to eight hours.

You shouldn't feel the cup once it's inside you. It can take some practice to get the positioning right, but once you figure it out, it can be a very comfortable option. You can then pull the cup out, and pour the blood down the toilet. You should rinse it under a tap before you insert it back in. Between each period, you have to clean it thoroughly – they come with instructions to explain how.

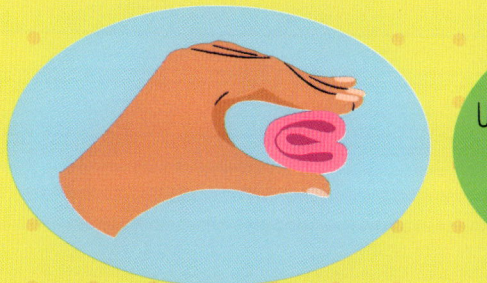
Pinch a menstrual cup to put it in.

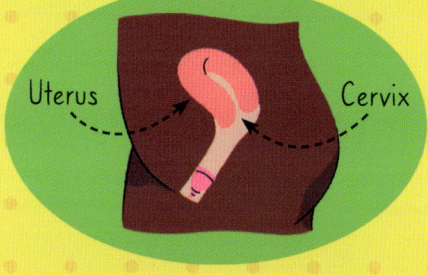
It unfolds inside your vagina.

MAKING YOUR DECISION

Some period products can seem daunting at first, but with a bit of practice you'll find what's best for you. It can also be helpful to talk through your options with a friend or adult.

PERIODS DAY TO DAY

Having periods is normal and healthy, but they can feel like a bit of a chore too. As you get older, you'll become familiar with your body and the things you can do to make that time of the month easier.

PERIOD PAIN

Some people get cramps below their tummy at the start of a period. This happens when muscles in the womb suddenly get tighter. Moving around, exercise, a warm bath or a hot water bottle over your cramps can ease the pain. You might find it helpful to take a painkiller. If your period pain stops you from taking part in your usual activities, then it might be worth speaking to a doctor.

BUSINESS AS USUAL

It's perfectly okay to slow down during your period to take extra care of yourself – your body is doing a lot of work! Over time, you'll find ways to manage your periods so that they become a normal part of your routine. They shouldn't stop you from doing all of the things that you enjoy.

BE PREPARED

It's helpful to note down the date your period begins, because it might come around at a similar time next month. Over time, you'll learn how to tell when a period is coming just by the way you feel. It's a good idea to carry period products with you when you're expecting a period, just in case.

Box or bag for tampons or pads

MOOD SWINGS

In the week leading up to a period, you may experience something called premenstrual syndrome (PMS). This can cause headaches, tiredness, tender breasts – and it can also make you feel moody, tearful or more sensitive than usual. Your emotions may change quite suddenly and you may not know why you feel a certain way.

Your brain, just like your body, is processing huge changes which can really impact how you feel. As your period comes and goes, your emotions will settle and you'll start to feel more like yourself again. You can read more about difficult emotions, and what causes them, on the next page.

FEELING HORMONAL

All of your emotions – feeling happy, sleepy, bored, hungry and more – are in part related to chemical messengers in your blood, called hormones. When it's time to start puberty, your brain tells your body to start producing all-new types of hormones, called sex hormones.

SEX HORMONES

Once your brain has sent the message to begin puberty, your body starts making three hormones in particular. They help your body to develop and grow in various ways.

Among other things, ESTROGEN causes your breasts to start growing.

PROGESTERONE helps your uterus shed a thick lining in the days before a period.

TESTOSTERONE helps to keep your bones healthy and give you energy.

A mix of these hormones also controls your period, and is what keeps them coming on a monthly cycle. In the days leading up to a period, your hormone levels change a lot. Getting used to these new hormones, and especially getting used to a monthly churn of hormones, can bring about big changes in your mood and energy levels.

MOOD SWING SURVIVAL GUIDE

As you get older, your hormones will settle down and, then, so will you. But in the meantime, there are plenty of things that you can do to help you cope with changing emotions.
Here are a few suggestions:

TAKE TIME OUT

Set aside time to do one thing you enjoy. It could be dancing to loud music, watching a movie or catching up with friends.

SCRIBBLE IT DOWN

Use a journal or notebook to write down how you're feeling. Putting things into words often helps process your emotions.

SPEAK TO SOMEONE

You might feel like shutting yourself away in your room – that's okay, but you don't always have to figure it out alone. Don't be afraid to ask for help if you're struggling to cope.

GO OUTSIDE

Being outside and doing exercise can boost your mood, making you feel happier and calmer.

YOU AND YOUR GENDER

Everyone changes as they grow, but the way you look on the outside is only part of the process. How you feel inside your head is really important too. It's partly to do with something called gender, and something else called sex. They're two different things.

Who am I?

YOUR BITS DOWN THERE

Your sex depends on the body bits you were born with. Most people are either male – with a penis – or female – with a vulva. When you were born, it's likely that a doctor looked at your genitals and said 'It's a girl!' or 'It's a boy!' But there's a lot more to it than that.

Gender is different from sex because it's about how you *feel*, rather than what body parts you have. You may feel like a boy, a girl, both or neither.

You might feel differently about your gender over time. It isn't a fixed thing, it can shift and change as you grow through puberty and into adulthood.

LABELS

Some people find it helpful to label the way their sex and gender do or don't line up. If your gender matches your sex, you are *cisgender*.

I was born with a vulva so I am considered female. I feel like a girl on the inside too! I'm cisgender.

If your gender doesn't match the body parts you were born with, then you might be *transgender* or *non-binary*:

I was born with a penis so I am considered male, but I don't feel like a boy! My sex and gender don't match.

There are labels for your sex, too. Roughly two out of every one hundred people are born with a mix of male AND female body parts. The technical name for this is being *intersex*. It's rare to see this just by looking. For example, if you have female genitals on the outside, but male genitals on the inside, you might not have any idea of being intersex until you hit puberty.

If you are intersex, it's common to start puberty later, and experience some changes but not others. This depends on the hormones swirling around inside you.

GENDER STEREOTYPES

It's pretty common, especially for grown-ups, to have ideas about what makes girls and boys different. This might be about what sorts of things one gender 'ought to' like, or how another gender 'ought to' behave. These are stereotypes, and they're often WRONG. Here are some examples of typical stereotypes about girls and boys.

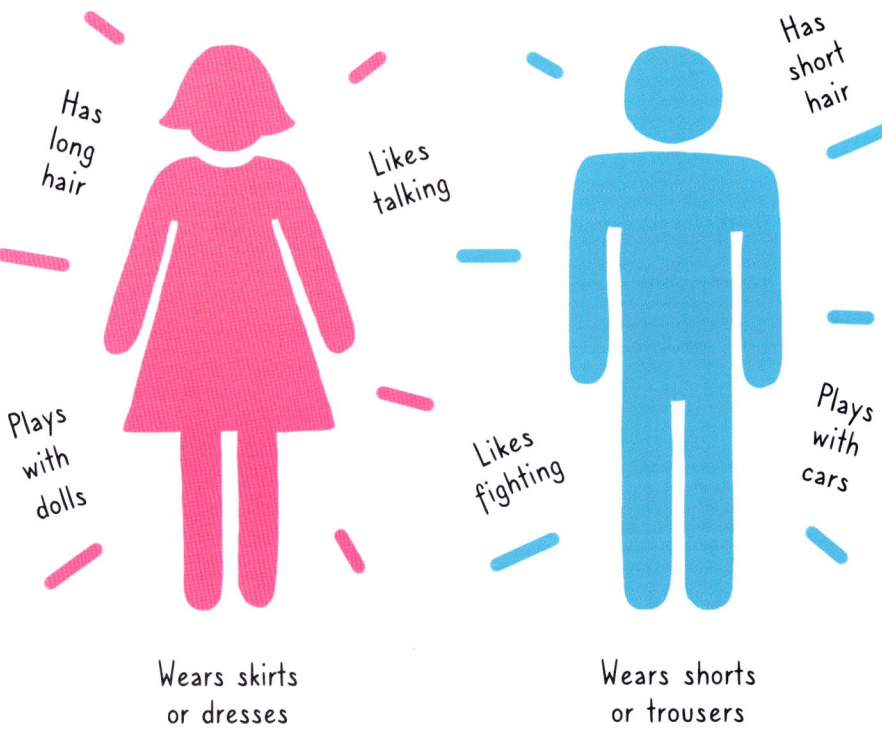

Wears skirts or dresses

Wears shorts or trousers

Some people do look and act in ways that fit a stereotype, but just as many people don't. Even if you can often correctly guess a person's *sex*, you can't tell a person's *gender* just by their face, or clothing, or what they're doing.

BEING YOURSELF

As you get older, you might start to feel pressure to be less childish and to act more like a grown-up. That sometimes includes people telling you to look and behave more like the stereotype THEY think is appropriate for your sex.

It can be tough if you don't want to dress or act in ways other people prefer. The fact is, there are many ways to be a boy or a girl – too many to make rules about. Equally, if you feel your sex doesn't match your gender, there are no rules about how you should look or act or dress to express your gender identity. It's enough just to be yourself.

I like wearing this T-shirt. The symbol stands for intersex representation.

I like sports and she likes dancing. And that's OK!

WHAT ABOUT BOYS?

Puberty isn't plain sailing for anyone, and boys are no exception. Although male bodies have different bits, and don't run on a monthly cycle, they still experience many of the same growing-up changes.

PRIVATE BITS

Here are the technical words for male genitals:

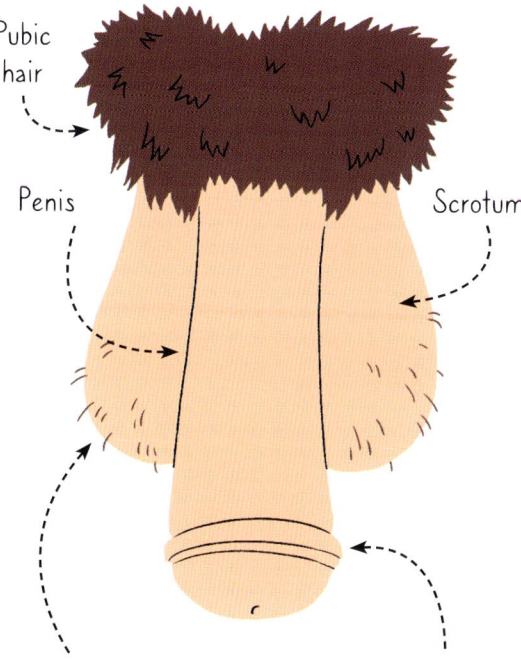

Pubic hair

Penis

Scrotum

Inside the scrotum are two balls called testicles. They make sex hormones and cells called sperm.

Foreskin – in some places and religions, this is cut away in a surgical operation called circumcision.

Just like vulvas, male body bits can be all different shapes and sizes.

A lot of boys spend a lot of time thinking and worrying about their penises. Sometimes it's because they think they're too small, or too bumpy, or are an odd shape. They're very sensitive to touch, and although they usually hang down between the legs, there are times when a penis will stiffen, get longer, and stick out...

I didn't ask for this to happen!

ERECTIONS

When a penis gets hard and sticks away from the body, it's called having an erection. It's caused by extra blood flowing into the penis.

Oh no, not again!

An erection can happen when a boy sees someone he has a crush on, or thinks about sex. And part of puberty, for many, is that they start to have crushes and think about sex more. But often, an erection seems to pop up for no reason at all.

It can feel extremely embarrassing if this happens in public, or if the bulge is tricky to hide. Usually, an erection goes away after a few minutes – but those minutes can feel like an age.

Some erect penises are straight, others bend to one side – all of them are normal.

EXPLORING YOUR BODY

When people are alone in private, they sometimes touch or rub their own genitals in a way that makes them feel good. This is known as masturbation, and it's a safe way to explore your body. When girls masturbate, their labia can swell up a little, their clitoris might get stiffer and their vagina may release some clear slippery fluid. It's something that lots of people do, often because it makes them feel good and relieves stress.

Anyone can masturbate, although not everybody wants to. Masturbation can lead to an orgasm – a happy, shuddering feeling that lasts a few seconds, also known as 'coming'. When boys have an orgasm, they usually also ejaculate. This is when a teaspoonful of white, gooey liquid, called semen, squirts or oozes out the end of their penis.

SEX DREAMS

It's possible to have an orgasm while you're asleep, during something known as a wet dream. You might be dreaming about sex, but not always. It's natural for this to happen, especially during puberty when your body is getting used to its new way of working. When a boy has a wet dream, he might ejaculate and get a wet patch on his pyjamas.

HAVING CRUSHES

You'll probably start to think in new ways as you get older. For example, you might start to have crushes on other people. This means a mix of things, such as thinking they're good-looking, or wanting to be around them, and hoping that they like *you*.

It's normal to feel excited or nervous when your crush is near. Having crushes is part of something called your sexuality, even though it's not always to do with sex. Some people find it helpful to give their sexuality a name – here are some examples.

BISEXUAL (Bi)
Attracted to people of more than one gender.

HETEROSEXUAL
Boys who are only attracted to girls, or girls who are only attracted to boys. Also known as being 'straight'.

PANSEXUAL
Attracted to other people, regardless of their gender, sex or sexuality.

HOMOSEXUAL
Attracted to people who are of the same sex or gender. Also known as being 'gay'. Gay girls often call themselves lesbians.

QUESTIONING
Someone who is questioning their sexuality, or curious about exploring other sexualities.

ASEXUAL
Not sexually attracted to anyone, but may or may not still feel romantically attracted to other people.

COMING OUT

People often wrongly assume that everyone is straight, unless they're told otherwise. Someone who isn't straight might choose to tell other people about their sexuality. This is known as 'coming out'. It's a personal decision if, when and how you choose to do it.

Some people are certain about their sexuality from a very young age, while other people discover more about themselves and get a better understanding of it over time. You can't choose your sexuality – it's just the way you are, and part of what makes you YOU.

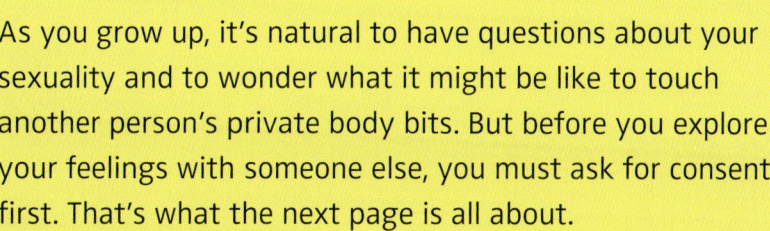

As you grow up, it's natural to have questions about your sexuality and to wonder what it might be like to touch another person's private body bits. But before you explore your feelings with someone else, you must ask for consent first. That's what the next page is all about.

YOUR BODY, YOUR RULES

Your body belongs to YOU. This means that nobody else can decide what you do with it. Before somebody touches you, they must first ask for your permission – this is called asking for consent.

Everyone is comfortable with different things, and it's important that we respect each other's boundaries. You can do this by asking for consent before you enter someone's personal space. Here are some examples of what this might look like:

THE RIGHT TO SAY NO

When someone asks YOU for consent, you can say yes, no or change your mind. You also don't need to give a reason – no means no. It's not okay for someone to pressure you into saying yes, or make you feel bad for saying no. And if you change your mind, they have to respect your decision. If you feel worried or scared, tell the person to stop, try to move away from them and tell an adult that you trust. You deserve to feel safe in your body.

CONSENT AND SEX

Sometimes people touch each other's private body bits. This is a different, more grown-up type of touching, but both people still need to give their consent first. It is against the law to touch anybody's private body bits without their permission, or for them to make you touch theirs. If this happens, it's not your fault and you should tell an adult. You might be curious to know what this grown-up touching is all about, so turn the page to find out.

WHAT ACTUALLY IS SEX?

Sex is when grown-ups touch the sensitive parts of each other's genitals in a way that might lead to an orgasm. This happens between people of all genders and for lots of different reasons. Some people have sex to show love and affection for each other – and because it feels good.

I thought sex was when a penis goes inside a vagina?

I thought sex was about making babies?

I thought sex was people getting naked and kissing and hugging.

Sex can be about all of those things!

BABY-MAKING SEX

People might also have sex in order to make a baby. This type of sex involves a penis going inside of a vagina. It typically happens like this...

First, two people kiss and cuddle each other closely. This is called foreplay, and it gets their bodies ready to have sex. The penis becomes erect, the vagina swells up slightly and releases some slippery fluid which helps the penis fit inside it. Both people move around, making the inside of the vagina rub against the outside of the penis. The penis ejaculates semen. The semen contains many millions of sperm, which are tiny cells that swim up through the vagina. If they meet an egg in the fallopian tubes, one of the sperm could join with it...

...and a baby may start growing.

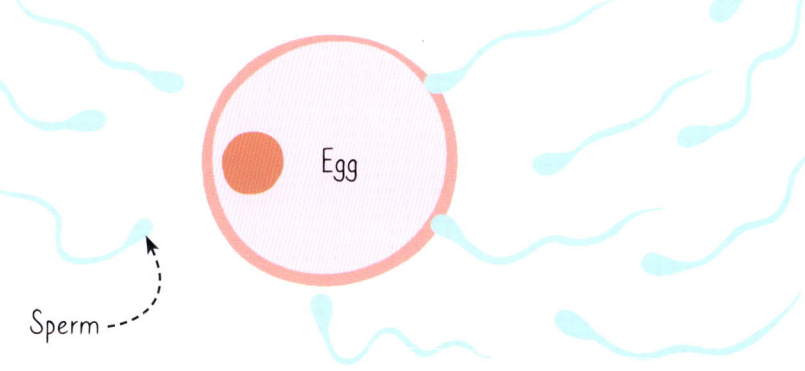

NOT JUST ABOUT BABIES

The idea of playing with other people's bits might seem weird. But lots of adults really like doing it, and one change that affects many teens during puberty is finding they want to do it, too. It's a common part of grown-up relationships. But in most places, it is against the law to have sex before the age of 16. This is known as the age of consent.

SAFE SEX

Sex comes with risks. One of those risks is getting pregnant, even if you don't want to. Another is catching or spreading disease. People can have sex with less risk of pregnancy, using something called contraception. To prevent spreading diseases, they use things called prophylactics.
There are several types.

One type is a condom – a thin rubber cover that goes over a penis before it enters a vagina. The end of the condom has a small bump which catches semen. This stops sperm from reaching the egg, and stops any diseases spreading, too.

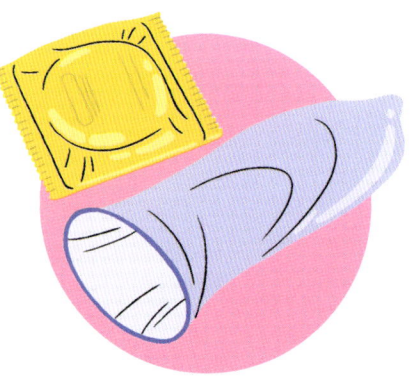

A condom comes in a wrapper, and can be unrolled onto the penis

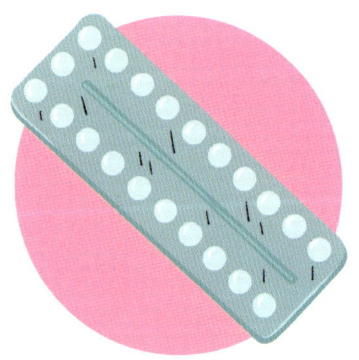

The contraceptive pill

Another method of contraception is the pill, which you can get from a doctor or pharmacy. You'd take one pill each day to stop your ovaries from releasing an egg. Some teenagers are also prescribed the pill to help with spots or very heavy periods.

There are other methods of contraception, but none are guaranteed to work every time.

SEX MYTHS

As you get older, you might notice that people start to talk about sex more and more. The chances are that some of what you hear isn't exactly true, especially when it comes to safe sex. Despite what people might tell you, you CAN get pregnant...

...even if it's your first time having sex.

...if the penis pulls out of the vagina before it ejaculates.

...while you are on your period.

...before you've had your first period.

...even if the penis doesn't go all the way in.

The only way to have safe sex is to use contraception.

AVOIDING INFECTIONS

There are some diseases that people can spread or catch when they have sex. These are called sexually transmitted infections, or STIs. Condoms are the only kind of contraception that also help prevent STIs. They act as a barrier that blocks infections from passing between people during sex.

BEING ONLINE

The internet is a great place to learn, play and connect with friends. But it's not without challenges. For example, it can be tempting to compare yourself to people you see and think that everyone else looks better or has a much more exciting life than you. That's rarely true – and here's why.

People only show a tiny portion of their lives online, and they only share the best bits. So what you're seeing isn't a realistic reflection of their day-to-day lives. Even the parts that are real aren't entirely true... because almost every image you see online has been edited, using filters or photoshop trickery. These can be very convincing, and the more you watch someone else's seemingly perfect, exciting, friend-filled life, the more it can make you feel lonely or insecure.

If you feel that happening, it's a good idea to come offline for a while and connect with your friends or family in person.

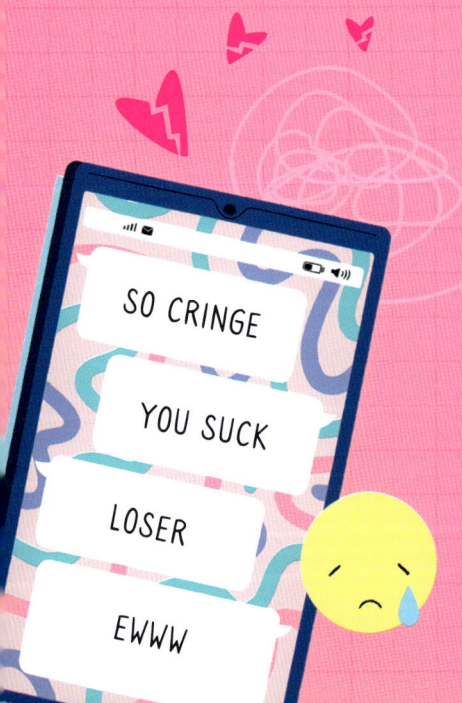

BATTLING TROLLS

People often say things online that they wouldn't say in person, including mean, hurtful things. That's called cyberbullying. Sometimes bullies do it to make you angry or sad, a nasty trick called trolling. It might be tempting to reply, but the best way to battle a troll is to ignore their message, or block them.

BODY IMAGE

Pictures of people online, especially filtered photos, can have a big impact on how you feel about yourself. Social media can make it seem as if you ought to look a certain way, which can make it difficult to feel confident.

Feeling happy with your body is called having a healthy body image. It is perfectly normal to have some insecurities, or to feel more confident on some days than others – everyone does.

But when someone worries about the way they look all the time, it means they have an unhealthy body image. They may struggle to look in a mirror without thinking of something they wish they could change. They may even develop dangerous habits, such as eating too little food. If you begin to feel this way, or think a friend feels this way, you should ask for help from an adult.

During puberty, your body will change a lot. On days when you might feel insecure, remember that there is no such thing as a perfect body. There are BILLIONS of people on Earth and each one is completely unique. A strong, healthy body can come in so many shapes and sizes. The way you look is just a small part of what makes you, YOU.

SEX ON THE INTERNET

At some point, you might come across videos or photos of people having sex or doing sexual things. This is called pornography, or porn, and it's a type of entertainment that is created ONLY for adults. Lots of young people are exposed to porn through the internet, long before they are ready to understand it.

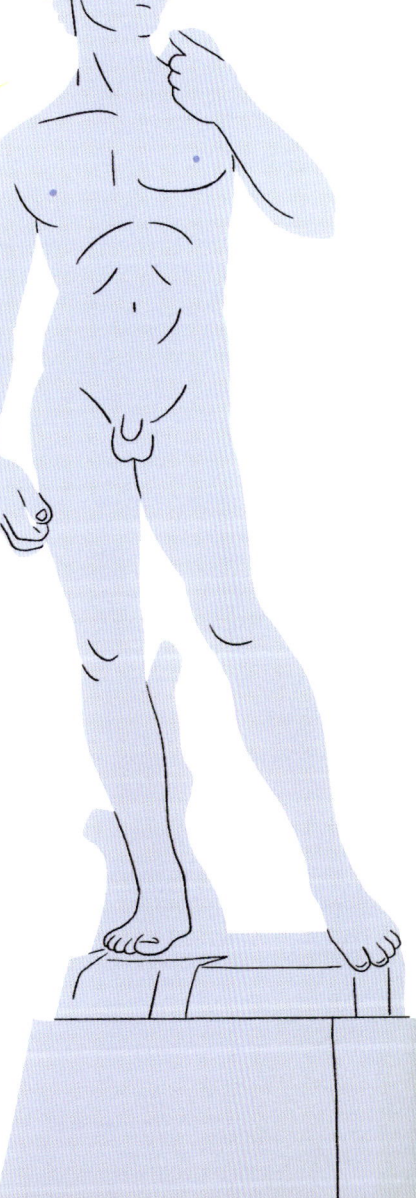

Not all naked pictures online are pornographic - they might be scientific diagrams, paintings or ancient statues like me!

Most countries have laws in place to restrict porn for people under a certain age (usually around eighteen). Parents, schools or companies can use filters to block it online, but some of it can still sneak through. Seeing porn might make you feel very uncomfortable, upset or scared. These feelings can be overwhelming, so you might find it helpful to speak to an adult you trust.

DON'T BELIEVE EVERYTHING YOU SEE

Most porn doesn't reflect what regular people look like, or how they act during sex. After all, people in porn aren't really having sex, they're *performing* sex, as actors. They do everything in a way that's easy for a camera to see, and it's often all planned out. They don't show what real sex looks like, and they're not role models for how you or anyone else is supposed to look or act during sex.

Looking at porn doesn't mean you're weird or a bad person. It's natural to be curious. But it's also completely normal if you haven't seen it, or don't want to. If a friend shows you porn, it's natural to feel embarrassed or overwhelmed. You can ask them to switch it off, or move away.

FUELLING YOUR BODY

During puberty, you need as much food as an adult because you're growing so fast. So eat when you feel hungry, and remember – putting on weight as a teenager is your body's way of storing energy for the changes ahead.

Eating a balanced diet will give you all the nutrients you need to feel healthy and energetic during the ups and downs of puberty. All 'balanced diet' means is getting a mix of different food types:

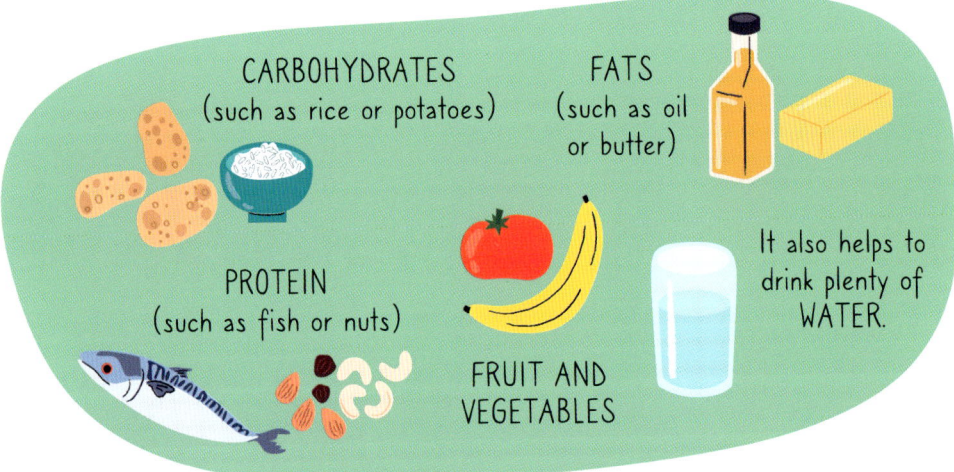

CARBOHYDRATES
(such as rice or potatoes)

FATS
(such as oil or butter)

PROTEIN
(such as fish or nuts)

FRUIT AND VEGETABLES

It also helps to drink plenty of WATER.

BREAKFAST

Try to make time for breakfast. Your body uses energy even while you're asleep and you need to replace it in the morning. A healthy breakfast stops you feeling weak and sluggish, improves your concentration and helps you function better all round.

BRUSHING YOUR TEETH

Most adult teeth have normally come through by the age of 13, and they will last you for life. To keep your teeth and gums healthy, you need to brush twice a day. If you have braces, it is a good idea to use interdental brushes to clean properly around each tooth.

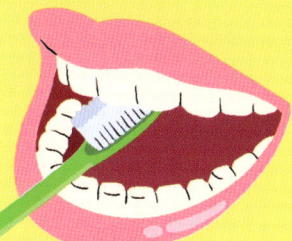

Angle your brush like this to clean the back of your teeth.

KEEP MOVING

Exercise is really good for your physical and mental health. It helps you to sleep well and feel more energetic. It also keeps your heart and bones healthy, which is especially important during puberty when your body is changing.

If you can, you should try to exercise for at least 150 minutes (2½ hours) a week. This sounds like a lot but you can split it into 10 minute bouts and can include walking to school.

Find a type of exercise that you enjoy. It doesn't have to be tiring. You just need to get your heart beating faster than normal for a few minutes.

Just as important, is to rest and get a good night's sleep. That's around 10 hours. Your body and your brain need this much sleep to keep healthy as you go through puberty.

KEEP CLEAN

You have sweat glands all over your skin, but there are more of them in some areas, such as your armpits and around your genitals. During puberty, you'll start to sweat more so it's a good idea to wash those bits every day.

Getting older and sweatier also means that you need to keep your clothes clean too. Clothes that sit close to your skin, such as socks, pants and T-shirts, pick up bacteria that loves sweat. So it's best to put them in the wash after each time you wear them.

SPOTS

Everyone's skin produces a kind of oil called sebum. Without it, your skin and hair would dry out. But changes in your hormone levels during puberty can increase it. Result: spots. They're totally normal, and everyone gets them from time to time. Wash your face once a day, and speak to a doctor if you get so many spots that it becomes difficult to manage.

CLEANING DOWN THERE

You DON'T need to clean inside your vagina. It's an amazing self-cleaner, so interfering with it could make you feel itchy or sore. But you DO need to wash your vulva. You only really need to use warm water for this – you can use a mild soap if you want to.

You should always wipe, wash and dry your genitals from front to back. This will stop germs spreading from your anus to your vagina or urinary tube, which can cause infections.

Dry here first.

Finish drying here.

NORMAL OR NOT?

You might notice white fluid coming out of your vagina. This is called discharge, and it keeps your vagina clean. There is more of it at some times than others and its colour can change from clear to milky-white. This is completely normal and healthy. It's only a problem if it starts to make you itch, burn or if it smells bad. This might mean you have an infection or an allergic reaction and you need to go to a doctor or pharmacist. It is likely they can help you without looking at your vagina.

OLDER AND WISER

One of the fun parts of puberty is gaining your independence. By the time you're grown up, you'll be able to make more decisions and take responsibility for yourself. This is really exciting! But it doesn't mean you can just do whatever you want all the time. You have to keep yourself safe.

CYBER SAFETY

You'll be told over and over again that you need to be safe online – it's boring, but it's true! The internet is an extremely helpful resource, but it comes with some risks. Create strong passwords to keep your accounts private, and don't share your full name, home address or the name of your school online. Before you post or share a photo, remember that you can never be sure who will see, save or forward it on. And most importantly, never chat to someone you don't know.

DRUGS

Drugs are chemicals that change the way your brain and body work, usually for a short time. When people talk about the dangers of drugs, they mostly mean illegal drugs such as ecstasy (a small pill) or cannabis (either a weed that people smoke, or a sweet they chew, known as 'edibles').

Vapes

Alcohol

Nitrous oxide

But actually the word 'drugs' includes other, legal, things that can be addictive and dangerous, such as pain-killing medicines and caffeine-heavy energy drinks.

Tobacco (in cigarettes), nicotine (in vapes) and alcohol are all addictive drugs that can be very bad for your health, especially when your body is developing. It's important to remember that all drugs affect each person differently, so you can never be sure how YOUR body will react to them.

Some people take drugs because they don't want to feel left out, or because they think it will make them look grown-up. It's important to remember that you shouldn't feel pressured to try something just to fit in – it's always okay to say no.

YOUR SUPPORT CREW

Family and friends can be a good source of support to help you through the tricky business of growing up. But during puberty, it's normal for these relationships, like everything else, to start to feel a bit different too.

AT HOME

It's not unusual to argue with your parents as you get older. When they make rules, it's often because they want the best for you. But it can still feel *very* frustrating when you disagree. Communicating your feelings calmly with the people close to you is a good way to set new boundaries as you mature. This might sound something like...

Please could you knock before coming into my room?

I know you're trying to help, but I'd like to figure this one out on my own.

I feel like I need some time alone if that's okay.

FRIENDSHIPS

It's normal for friendship groups to shift around during puberty as people develop new interests and mature at different rates. True friends will value you for who you really are, so you shouldn't feel pressured to change in order to fit in with a group.

You might feel as though everyone is looking at you, or worry about what other people think. Scientists call this an imaginary audience, and everyone experiences it. If you feel self-conscious, it might be helpful to remember that people around you want to fit in too, and most likely don't notice what you're wearing or how you look.

BECOMING YOU

Try to think of people you admire – they could be people you know in real life or celebrities you find inspiring. Having positive role models you can relate to is a great way to motivate yourself, and to help you imagine what sort of grown-up you'd like to be.

Discovering who you are takes time, and it's not something that stops after puberty. Your identity will shift and change throughout your life, so you don't need to have everything figured out right away. Take time to experiment with clothes, listen to different styles of music, try your hand at new hobbies and meet lots of new people. It's your life – enjoy it!

GLOSSARY

Words written in *italic* type are defined in their own entry.

Clitoris Sensitive, pea-shaped bump near the top of the *vulva*
Coming out When a person tells someone else about their *sexuality*
Condom A method of *contraception* that goes over the *penis* to stop *sperm* getting into the *vagina*. Also prevents STIs spreading
Consent Asking for permission before touching another person
Contraception Methods used to stop someone getting *pregnant* when *having sex*
Contraceptive pill A method of *contraception* that works by taking a pill each day, often just called 'the pill'
Discharge White or milky fluid that keeps the *vagina* clean
Drugs Pills, liquids, powders and gases that temporarily change the way your brain and body feel, often addictive and dangerous
Eggs Tiny parts of the body made in the *ovaries*. Each month, one egg comes out of one ovary. It comes out of the *vagina* as a *period*, unless it fuses with *sperm* to become a baby
Ejaculation When *semen* comes out of the *penis*
Erection When extra blood flows into the *penis*, making it hard or stiff
Gender How a person identifies themself, for example as being male, female, or both, or neither
Gender stereotypes The mistaken idea that some people should act or look a certain way because of their *gender*
Genitals Your private body bits that are in between your legs
Hormones Chemical messages in your blood that tell your body to do different things, such as starting *puberty*
Intersex Someone born with a mix of male and female *sex organs* and *hormones*, often impossible to tell just by looking
Masturbation When someone rubs or touches their own *genitals* in a way that might lead to an orgasm
Orgasm A shuddering, happy feeling that people may get when their

genitals are touched or rubbed. It usually lasts a few seconds, also known as 'coming'

Ovaries Part of the female *sex organs* where *eggs* are stored

Penis Part of the male *genitals* that hangs down in between the legs

Period A time when the lining of the *uterus* comes out of the *vagina* as period blood for a few days each month

Period products Things you can use to soak up *period* blood, such as tampons, pads, cups and period pants

PMS (Premenstrual syndrome) Feeling sad, irritated or anxious in the days leading up to a *period*

Pornography Grown-up videos or images of people being naked, *having sex*, or touching each other's private body bits

Pregnancy When a *sperm* fuses with an *egg* which causes a baby to start growing in the *uterus*

Puberty When the body starts making lots of new *hormones* that bring about growing-up changes

Semen A white, gooey fluid containing *sperm* that can come out of the *penis* during *ejaculation*

Sex The word sex is used to mean two different things:
 1. The body bits a person is born with – typically female, male or intersex
 2. 'Having sex' is when people touch each other's *genitals* in a way that might make an *orgasm* happen

Sex organs Parts of the body related to *having sex* and making babies

Sexuality A word used to describe either the type of people you're attracted to, or that you don't feel attracted to anyone

Sperm Tiny body parts found in *semen* that can lead to a baby being made, if one of them fuses with an *egg*

Testicles Part of the male *sex organs* where *sperm* is made

Uterus (womb) Part of the female *sex organs* where a baby can grow

Vagina The opening to a tube inside your body where discharge and *period* blood comes out

Vulva The name for the female body bits between the legs

Wet dream When a dream leads to an *orgasm* during sleep

INDEX

body positivity, 47
bones, 7, 16, 28, 51
boys, 34-37
brain, 28-29, 51, 55
breasts, 10-13, 18, 27, 28
bullying, 46

cervix, 17, 23, 25
clitoris, 14-15, 37
coming out, 39
consent, 39-41, 43
contraception, 44-45

discharge, 17, 53
drugs, 55

eggs, 17, 43, 44
ejaculation, 37, 43, 45
emotions, 27-29
erections, 36, 43
exercise, 13, 26, 29, 51

fallopian tubes, 17, 43
food, 47, 50-51

gender, 30-33, 38
genitals, 14-15, 30-31, 34-37, 42-43
growth spurt, 6

hair, 8-9, 14-15, 34-35, 52
hormones, 28-29, 31, 35, 52
hymen, 14

infections, 23, 45, 53
intersex, 31, 33

labia, 14-15, 37

masturbation, 37
muscles, 7, 26

orgasms, 37, 42
ovaries, 17, 44

penis, 30-31, 34-37, 42-45
periods, 17-28, 44-45
period products, 20-25, 27
PMS, 27
pornography, 48-49
pregnancy, 18, 42-45
puberty, 3-5, 28, 34
pubic hair, 8, 15, 34, 35

safe sex, 44-45
semen, 37, 43, 44
sex, 36-38, 41-45, 48-49
sex and gender, 30-33, 38
sex organs, 14, 16-17, 35
sexuality, 38-39
sleep, 23, 51
sperm, 35, 43, 44
spots, 44, 52
STIs, 45

uterus, 16-18, 23, 25, 28

vagina, 14, 17-19, 22-23, 25, 37,
    42-45, 53
vulva, 14-15, 30-31, 53

weight, 4, 7, 50
wet dreams, 37